The

Platinum

Rule

by

Art Fettig

Art Fettig's
Growth Unlimited Inc.

Dedicated to helping people grow
Up!
Up!
Up!

36 Fairview, Battle Creek, MI 49017
(800) 441-7676 (616) 965-2229 Fax (616) 965-4522

Printed in Canada

Library of Congress
Catalog Number 87-081732
Fettig, Art
The Platinum Rule
ISBN-0-916927-09-1

Books and Booklets by Art Fettig

Safety Books

Selling Safety In The 90's
World's Greatest Safety Meeting Idea Book
More Great Safety Meeting Ideas Book
A Declaration Of Interdependence For Safety Booklet *
A Personal Pledge To Safety *
You Do WHAT While You Drive? *
How To Use The Book, "How Funny Art You, The Humor Game"
To Build Great Safety Teams
Winning The Safety Commitment

Sales Books

Selling Lucky
Selling Luckier Yet
16 Great Lucky Selling Ideas *
World's Greatest Sales Meeting Idea Book
How To Follow-Up! For Greater Success In Sales
Seeing Your Book In print *

Speaking Books

How To Hold An Audience In The Hollow Of Your Hand
Anatomy Of A Speech *
Showtime
How Funny Are You?
Speaking, Speaking *
Como Meterse Al Publico En El Bolsillo

Inspirational Books

Reflection On Growth Booklet *
Self-Esteem Credo Booklet *
Love Is The Target
Mentor: Secrets Of The Ages

The Platinum Rule
Serenity! Serenity!
This Is It! *
Songwriter

Parent's Teacher's Books

It Only Hurts When I Frown
The Pos Parenting Book
The Declaration Of Interdependence For Excellence *

Children's Books

The Three Robots
The Three Robots Learn About Drugs
The Three Robots Find A Grandpa
The Three Robots Discover Their Possibilities
The Three Robots And The Sandstorm
Remembering
The Pos Activity Book
The New Just Say Yes Activity Book
The Santa Train *

Novels

Unfit For Glory
Success Rally

Business

Welcome To The 21st Century *

Verses

Army Memoirs 1952 *
A Single Man At Burnham Brook *
A Special Collection Of Verses For Seniors *
Best Verses Of Art Fettig And Friends *

For a complete catalog of Art Fettig Books and Tapes
contact

Growth Unlimited Inc.
36 Fairview Ave
Battle Creek, MI
49017

Phone: (800) 441-7676
Fax: (616) 965-4522
Email: artfettig@voyager.net
Website: www.IMASource.com

Dedication

To all of the wonderful people I've met who have already discovered the awesome power of the *Platinum Rule* by practicing it in their lives. And to all those who will discover the *Platinum Rule* and have the courage and the heart to practice it.

The Gift of Giving

by W. Clement Stone

Be generous! Give to those you love; give to those who love you; give to the fortunate; give to the unfortunate——yes, give especially to those to whom you don't want to give. You will receive abundance for your giving. The more you give, the more you will have!

Give a smile to everyone you meet (smile with your eyes) and you'll receive smiles.

Give a kind word (with a kindly thought behind the word) and you will receive kind words.

Give appreciation (warmth from the heart) and you will be appreciated.

Give time for a worthy cause (with eagerness) and you will be richly rewarded.

Give hope (the magic ingredient for success) and you will be made hopeful.

Give happiness and you will be made happy.

Give encouragement (the incentive to action) and you will be encouraged.

Give prayers (the instrument of miracles) and you will receive blessings.

–Excerpted by permission from PMA Adviser, April 1984.

In his book *The Wickman Formula, Seven Steps to Achieving Your Full Potential*, Floyd Wickman, CEO of a multimillion dollar corporation, tells of how he had just dictated his corporate philosophy, expanding on his corporate motto, "We get by giving," when he first received a copy of *The Platinum Rule*.

Now Floyd encourages his employees and members of his many audiences not only to practice the Platinum Rule in their personal lives but in their business practices as well.

"Art Fettig has identified a little known key to wealth and happiness in his book *The Platinum Rule*. I hope that millions of people discover this little book and apply this giving formula. Truly their lives will be enriched and certainly this will be a better world."

The Wickman Formula, Executive Press 1991

"You may never have the opportunity to spend 24 hours with 'Mr. Platinum' as I was so fortunate to do - but you do have the opportunity to read his book and Go Platinum yourself. *The Platinum Rule* has changed my life, my wife's life, and the lives of most of the people whom I'm surrounded by. I know it can do the same for you!"

- Ralph R. Roberts
President & Founder, Ralph R. Roberts Real Estate, Inc.
Author of *Walk Like a Giant, Sell Like a Madman*
(Harper Business)
Named "the best selling realtor in America" by TIME magazine

Ralph R. Roberts Real Estate Inc.
30521 Schoenherr
Warren, MI 48093

810-751-0000
24-hour Infoline 800-704-5189
www.ralphroberts.com

Foreword

A wise person once said, "You can only keep what you give away and you can only enjoy what you share." These two great truths lie dormant in everyone until they are brought to life through reading a book, meeting a special person, or by a special heart experience. Art Fettig shares in this book how these truths became a reality in his life.

Art credits me as the person that helped him discover the HOW of "Give to Get". Art practices the principles of greatness by always giving credit, which reminds me that I too need to give credit to the one who helped me make the same discovery. It was an old retired pastor, Tracy C. Miller. Until I met him I thought I should give to get things.

This old teacher with his love for God and His word, helped me see that if I give only to get, I am trading. But if I give because I have, I get something better than things, I get a greater capacity to give more. Of course the wise old pastor shared with me the one who taught this principle more beautifully than any other, Jesus Christ. "For God so loved the world, that He gave His only begotten Son, that whosoever believeth in Him should not perish, but have everlasting life."

I hope this short book will have an everlasting effect on your life as you discover the meaning of this great law of love & life.

Charles "Tremendous" Jones

The Platinum Rule

 WAS IN WESTERN SPAIN IN A SMALL town called Tauvillo. During a wonderful day visiting with my daughter, Amy, and her husband Roosevel, we traveled the winding mountains and then met with Roosevel's sister, Martha, her husband, Arturo, and their two boys, Arturo, Jr., and Alverto.

We were walking upstairs from the bar to the dining room of the restaurant, Las Ciguenas, and I had a few coins in my pocket. So when we walked past a slot machine, I motioned to the group that I wanted to try my luck.

    I inserted a 25 peseta coin and Arturo, Jr.
gave a good crank on the slot's handle. Arturo is
just nine, but still he pulled the crank like an
experienced gambler.

    Three lights signalled that I had a chance
to push other buttons in an effort to make three
of a kind, and Martha motioned everyone back
from the machine. "Automatic," she said and we
all waited until a timer in the machine triggered
the automatic select device. Finally, the machine
started clicking and the revolving fruits and bells
on the slots moved forward, stopping with 3 bells
up.

The machine began to celebrate its own wise decision by making a loud exciting noise and spitting out a pile of 25-peseta coins onto the tray below. The payoff was 400 pesetas, sixteen to one.

After dinner I gave all of the coins back to the machine with a few of my own for good measure.

Slot machines are really not a good way for one to seek one's fortune. I have discovered a much safer way which I will share with you.

The greatest pleasure I know is to do a good action
by stealth, and to have it found out by accident.

Charles Lamb

Most who read these words will not com-
prehend the power of my message. And of those
who might understand it, fewer yet will take the
actions which are suggested.

I, myself, have known this powerful life-changing secret for some time, yet, only recently have I dared to give the process a real try.

Let me begin by telling you that my search for the true meaning of this secret began one day several years ago when I read a brief item written by W. Clement Stone in his magazine **Success**.

In the article, Mr. Stone stated briefly that one of his favorite books was **Magnificent Obsession** by Lloyd C. Douglas.

W. Clement Stone, by the way, is a Chicago businessman reported to now be worth many, many millions of dollars. His known philanthropies are legend and God alone knows the true extent of his giving.

In the book, **Success Through A Positive Mental Attitude** which Mr. Stone co-authored, a whole chapter was devoted to revealing the secret contained in the book **Magnificent Obsession** and attesting to its power.

Magnificent Obsession is a novel that was first published in 1929. This piece of fiction has proven to be a very popular work. In the book a man named Dr. Wayne Hudson dies and leaves behind a strange diary written in code.

As the two central figures in the book seek to decipher this code, they discover the meaning of this powerful secret which had dramatically altered the life of Dr. Hudson.

The story reveals how Dr. Hudson had learned this secret from a great sculptor who had struggled as an unskilled workman chiseling names on grave markers.

Yet, once this sculptor learned the secret and put it to work in his life, his talents increased to the point where his work became world renowned.

Dr. Hudson changed from a self-serving failure who had little interest in his medical profession, to a loving man who became outstanding in his field.

This life-changing secret is so simple and easy to apply that you might think it foolish of me to claim such great powers for it. Yet because most humankind has become so self-serving, this process might appear to demand a great sacrifice on your part.

Be assured, the investment you must make is a great one which might very well, in time, claim all of your time, all of your talents and all of your wealth.

By then though, be assured, your surplus will be so great and your heart so full that it will be of little matter.

Sometimes a man imagines that he will lose himself if he gives himself, and keep himself if he hides himself. But the contrary takes place with terrible exactitude.

Ernest Hello, Life, Science, and Art

Once, in Arizona, I had the opportunity to visit with Og Mandino, the famous author of many great books such as **The Greatest Miracle** and **The Greatest Salesman**. I shared with Og my belief that most of the truly great pieces of fiction were really great truths cloaked in fiction wherein the characters go through their struggles to learn those truths. Certainly this was true of all of Og Mandino's books.

It is true of my own book, **Mentor—Secrets Of The Ages**. It is also true of the **One Minute Manager** by Doctors Ken Blanchard and Spencer Johnson, and all of the other **One Minute** series of best sellers.

When I shared this with Og Mandino, he seemed to truly enjoy the idea.

"That is important what you have learned, Art," Og said. "Be sure and write your discovery so that others might benefit from it."

I suggested to Og that each of us could probably summarize the great truths from our books on little cards. Then running from reader to reader, we might say, "Here it is. Here's the great truth which will change your life. It is so simple you can read it in just a moment."

And most would just look at the card and say, "It isn't much. It must not be very important."

And so we cloak these truths in fiction and let the reader struggle along with our make-believe characters hoping that perhaps a few of our readers will learn the life-changing secrets; secrets which have come into our lives and make them better.

Lloyd C. Douglas shared with the readers of **Magnificent Obession** a truth so powerful that the reader might attain great fame, great wealth, great power and, even more important, great happiness and personal fulfillment by applying this knowledge.

Now if I simply tell you that secret, it will, no doubt, be like writing a great truth on a little card and giving it to you, saying, "Here is the secret to greatness in whatever profession you care to venture. Here is the key to untold fortune and happiness."

It would be a risk to tell you the secret at this time. And yet, I will...

When the giver comes, the gate opens by itself.

> *German Proverb*

First find someone with a special need. I am not talking about those who are perpetually in need. What you are looking for is someone who has a temporary need. In the **Magnificent Obsession**, it was often someone in need of funds for surgery. It might be someone in need of a special training or perhaps a trip.

Consider finding the right person and the right situation for your circumstances.

It is very difficult to explain the recruiting system because once you put your mind to this process, believe me, the person and the situation will quickly appear.

My own difficulty with the process is that somehow I had the idea in my head that it was simply a financial commitment.

I soon discovered that the undertaking which I embarked upon involved not only my money but my time and talents as well.

Fortunately, I found great joy in the doing. In addition to the immediate happiness which I experienced, I realized a remarkable increase in my talents and in my financial returns.

A charitable man is like an appletree—He gives his fruit and is silent; the philanthropist is like the hen.

Author Unknown

Having found the right person and situation, the rest is quite simple.

You must require of them a vow of secrecy. They must never reveal to anyone else that you were their benefactor. And you must promise the same to them.

Secrecy is the real key to the success of this unique process.

He who gives to me teaches me to give.

Danish Proverb

Finally, the receiving party must also understand that under no circumstances will he or she ever attempt repayment of your gift. Once given by you, that resource has served its purpose in your life and it is not to be returned.

Perhaps the receiving party might, at some time in his or her life, find him/herself in a position to pass such a kindness on to yet another party, but that is their decision to make.

Your payment is in the joy of giving.

Maybe we could draw an analogy. Think for a moment of a giant steam locomotive pulling 120 freight cars. Imagine that it would take 100% of that locomotive's power to get that long, heavy train moving.

Now consider that same locomotive with just 97% of the power necessary to get the train underway. Once underway, of course, that same train would require but a small fraction of its power to keep moving. Let us say, perhaps just 3%.

A similar analogy might be drawn to a rocket on a launching pad. Imagine for a moment, a rocket with just 97% of the thrust power required to go into orbit. Once in orbit it would again require but a small fraction of the power to remain in orbit.

You can provide the momentum to change a person's life.

The more one gives, the more one has to give—like milk in the breast.

Anne Morrow Lindbergh, *Gift from the Sea*

I don't expect you to take any dramatic action at first. I don't expect you to take any action at all because most of us are not brought up that way.

You see, I want you to give up 20% of all you now have and 20% of all you will obtain in the future.

Please do not conclude that what I am proposing should be done through a church or a religious organization. Certainly you should follow the dictates of your faith and your heart in this regard. Personally, I think this secret that we are sharing is not restricted to just one belief. It appears to work for most who generously commit.

17

And it is not only your wealth which I want you to share. I want you to share 20% of your time, 20% of your talents and 20% of your whole being.

There, now I know that I've lost you. No doubt your immediate response is, "I cannot afford to give up 20% of what I have. I have barely enough to survive on right now."

What if I increased your net worth tenfold? Could you then afford to give up 20%? Probably not.

And what if I increased your net worth a hundredfold? Could you then afford to give 20%?

So many people look at the world's greatest givers and say, "Sure, if I had that kind of money, I'd be a philanthropist too."

And yet, I am suggesting that those who give this way have great worth because they learned the secret of giving.

What I have just discovered is that many of the world's greatest philanthropists were philanthropists when they had nothing.

It could well be that these philanthopists attained their great fortunes because they truly understood and practiced the secret which I am sharing with you.

I am sure that by now you might be thinking, "This guy is some kind of a nut who is affiliated with one of those TV preachers."

"He probably wants us to sell our homes and our cars and mail in the proceeds so that another religious TV show might stay on the air for another week."

Not so!

I have no special interest in the way you use the information that I'm sharing with you.

Frankly, I don't expect to create a great following by sharing this secret.

Most who are exposed to this powerful rule for untold fortune, will shrug their shoulders, shake their heads slowly and decide, "I can't afford such an experiment. What if I failed? I would be out too much," or, "Perhaps some day when money and time and effort no longer mean anything— then perhaps I will give it a try just for my amusement."

And others will nod and say, "Yes, we believe you and no doubt it would work if only we made a serious effort, but the time is not right for us. We will try it some day when we have more time to devote to the experiment."

Of course what you are actually saying and what I hear you saying are two distinctly different things.

What I hear you saying is that you are too engrossed in failure at the present time to be encumbered with true success and happiness.

A man there was, though some did count him mad. The more he cast away the more he had.

John Bunyan, Pilgrim's Progress

A number of years ago a very successful insurance salesman read the book **Magnificent Obsession** and it impressed him so that he asked his wife to read it too. When she finished reading the book he proposed that they devote a percentage of their income and time, in fact of their whole lives, to the magnificent quest of helping others. After a lot of reflection, they both came up with the figure 40%.

I can now report to you that that 40% figure must have been the right one because this fellow is a lifetime member of the Million Dollar Roundtable, a fairly select group of the top insurance people in the world. Much more than that though, he is a highly respected member of his community. He has attained what most people would consider great wealth.

Both he and his wife have shared a wonderful life and by all of the standards that I know of, he and his wife are outstanding successes.

Ask him the secret of his success and he will tell you about his favorite book, **Magnificent Obsession.**

My friend did not follow the exact script of the book. In many instances he worked through organizations, committees, projects with formal structures. What he did do, though, was commit 40% of his entire life to serving people. That attitude and philosophy rubbed off in all his business dealings.

When I give, I give myself

Walt Whitman

Now let me borrow from a great truth once explained to me by a friend, Charles T. Jones.

He explains it well when he says, "You must give to get." And he repeats it again and again. "Give to get. Give to get. Give to get." and then he clarifies it somehow by saying, "You give to get but you do not give to get."

Are you thoroughly confused? I was for some time.

Finally Charlie got through to me by explaining, you must give to get. That is simply the way life works. It is a rule that never changes.

However, if you want to get any joy out of life then you must learn to give simply for the joy of giving. You will then get, automatically.

But, when you give so that you will get, you are no longer giving. Then you are trading. Trading spoils the whole process.

I said before that the process demands that you discover the right person and situation and initiate a vow of secrecy between you.

Then the other party must thoroughly understand that repayment is not only unnecessary, but forbidden.

Quite simple? Uncomplicated? Disappointing?

So often we expect great truths to be complicated and yet I have most often found that the great truths that I have learned are, once learned, so simple that one wonders why their meaning eludes most of us throughout our lifetime.

As I said earlier, I could have written this powerful formula for great talent and great fortune on a little card and given it to you. Then you would probably say "It is so simple it couldn't be worth much." And you would probably ignore it and give it no further thought.

I mentioned Charles T. Jones as a man who taught me the formula for discovering joy in giving. Well, as it turned out, he is also responsible for my finally applying that wonderful secret I first discovered in reading **Magnificent Obsession.**

You see, Charles T. Jones is one of the world's truly great professional speakers. He has had a great influence on my own speaking style.

One day I received a letter from Charlie asking me to contribute just one page to a book he was putting together.

Charlie is a man who understands the power of great books and he spends a great part of his life persuading people to read more.

The book he was preparing was a collection of one-page articles by the many authors with whom Charlie was acquainted. He asked each of us to describe one book which had truly influenced our lives. Now for some time I had been thinking about the conversation I'd had with Og Mandino when he had suggested I write down what I had discovered about how authors cloak great truths in fictional plots, allowing their characters to struggle with life as bit by bit, they learn these great truths.

The moment that I received Charlie's request, I immediately knew that this was my opportunity to write what Og Mandino had suggested. And what better book to write about than **Magnificent Obsession,** the very book which had revealed this writing process to me?

Within a week Charlie had my writing in his hands, and a short time after that I received a note from Charlie thanking me and accepting my contribution for his book. It was just six months or so later when I received the book containing my article.

The response from Charlie's request to authors for writing contributions was so great that Charlie soon had three books in publication.

Within a few months of publication, I began hearing from friends and strangers alike, saying that they had read my writing in Charlie's book.

They would smile knowingly, nod and say, "So you know the secret too!"

Some of them would share other books with me that somehow touched upon the subject of this great secret.

Some were more mystic approaches referring to the production of psychic energy. They indicated that once you provided that extra necessary 3 or 4 percent to move that locomotive or put the rocket in a person's life into orbit, then you might draw psychic energy thereafter from that person's excess.

Another book was of the "send me ten dollars and I will send you the secret to becoming a millionaire" type. Although the message was based on greed, still it contained several of the necessary ingredients of this marvelous secret.

One friend gave me a copy of another of Lloyd C. Douglas' books titled, **Dr. Hudson's Secret Journal.** This was a sequel to the book **Magnificent Obsession.**

In the preface of the book the author tells how he had truly written a book of fiction and had created the secret which he shares in the book. It was not a process that he truly believed in, but one which he had created in his imagination.

The book was an immediate success, soon becoming a best seller. Once released, the author began receiving thousands of letters from readers who had applied this secret in their own lives.

A few complained that they had tried the formula and that it had failed, and they were greatly upset to have squandered their money.

But the vast majority who wrote told of the increase in talents, and wealth, and happiness which had come into their lives.

After awhile I realized that those people who were approaching me and sharing the fact that they too knew the secret, were the most successful and financially sound people of my acquaintance. It was obvious that the secret was working great wonders in their lives.

The only gift is a portion of thyself.

Emerson, "Gifts," Second Series

One evening during that time in my life, I received a telephone call from a woman who is the financial manager of a very famous family that has been widely successful with their music on TV, movies, records and with shows in Las Vegas. I will not mention their name because they realize, too, that giving is best kept secret.

I took the opportunity to ask her, "Tell me, what is the secret to your family's success?"

Without hesitation she stated, "We tithe."

I was not satisfied with her answer and so I said, "But many people tithe, yet they are not as talented nor as successful as your family. What else is the secret?" And she replied, "We tithe 20%"

Again I pressed on, "Come on, surely there is more to that secret. Tell me what else is the secret to your family's outstanding success."

And she replied, "We tithe 20% of our gross income."

That conversation was a revelation to me. I understood the word "tithe" to mean 10%. I questioned myself, if we give for the joy of giving and then as an after-effect we get, then might not the answer to abundance be the abundance of giving?

If we doubled up on our giving would our joy be doubled or might the law of reciprocity have a multiplying effect?

Could the key to great abundance be contained in great, controlled, secret giving?

It is well to give when asked, but it is better to give unasked, through understanding.

Kahlil Gibran, "On Giving," The Prophet

In II Corinthians 9:4-6 you will find, "but remember this—if you give little, you will get little." A farmer who plants just a few seeds will get only a small crop, but if he plants much, he will reap much.

Everyone should make his own decision as to how much he should give. Don't force anyone to give more than he really wants to. "For cheerful givers are the ones God prizes." (II Corinthians 9:7) God is able to make it up to you by giving you everything you need and more.

So there will not only be enough for your own needs, but plenty left over to give joyfully to others.

Certainly this is what we have been discussing right along, but let me explain that I am a slow learner.

If I were asked to name my greatest asset, I must confess that it is my slowness in learning combined with my overpowering persistence to learn.

I plow into a subject with such a dim wit and a rare tenacity that, once understood, I can explain a truth so that a five-year-old child will understand too.

I have been accused of writing adult books for children and children's books for adults. And so it is that I must be exposed to a great truth again and again, and again, and only then might I hope to understand and apply that truth to my life.

Charity should link us together by the very thing which divides or distinguishes us.

Anthony G. Sertillanges, *Rectitude*

The next stage of my learning came with a visit to California.

For some time I had been corresponding with an editor of Christian books. He had been an editor with a Christian publisher at the time when I submitted a still unpublished work of mine titled, **Reborn Again.** He had been kind enough to write me and explain that my work was interesting but that somehow the book was not right.

41

What he was saying was that my faith and understanding of Jesus Christ was not yet strong enough.

I talked with him a number of times on the phone and then he left that publisher and moved on.

It was a few years later when he wrote me saying that he was now with a different Christian publishing house and he was just inquiring how my life was going and how my faith was growing. Since I was planning a trip to California, I wrote and asked if I might visit him at his office.

I drove from my daughter's home at El Cajon, near San Diego, to San Bernardino and he and I had a wonderful visit.

Later, as I read one of the books my friend had given me, I came upon a section which explained that difference between a Carnal Christian and a Spiritual Christian.

The Carnal Christian was self-centered, allowing Christ to play only a secondary role in his or her life. On the other hand, the Spiritual Christian puts Christ first.

As I read on I learned that a Christ-centered person is drawn to the Bible and finds great joy in reading the word of God.

Since that time, I have made an even greater commmitment to Christ in my life. I sought to read the entire New Testament, for the first time.

In my fifty some years of life I had attempted to read the Bible perhaps a dozen times with no success at all. Now I was afire and armed with a new, easily understandable version of the Bible and I tried once again. This time everything was different.

Suddenly the Bible was one of the greatest books I had ever read. Great truths were now becoming very clear to me as I experienced a new sense of happiness.

It was while reading Matthew that a very strange thing occurred.

Although the Bible had been most interesting to me thus far, as I got to Matthew 4:21-22, I was suddenly quite bored. I read this section again and again and still it had little meaning to me.

I felt a very strong impulse to skip ahead a few chapters and after several attempts to resist this temptation I finally gave in and read Matthew 6:1-8. It said:

"Take care! Don't do your good deeds publicly, to be admired, for then you will lose the reward
from your Father in Heaven. When you give a gift
to a beggar, don't shout about it as the hypocrites
do—blowing trumpets in the synagogues and
streets to call attention to their acts of charity! I tell
you in all earnestness, they have received all the
reward they will ever get. But when you do a
kindness to someone, do it secretly—don't tell your
left hand what your right hand is doing. And your
Father who knows all secrets will reward you."

"And now about prayer. When you pray,
don't be like the hypocrites who pretend piety by
praying publicly on street corners and in the
synagogues where everyone can see them. Truly,
that is all the reward they will ever get. But when
you pray, go away by yourself, all alone, and shut
the door behind you and pray to your Father secretly, and your Father, who knows your secrets, will
reward you."

Here again was that very message contained in **Magnificent Obsession.** The impor-
tance of secrecy in your charity.

The moment that others discover your good
deeds, that discovery, itself, is your reward.

I thought about all of the generous people
in this world who make the largest donations to
the United Way to great applause.

I thought of the givers who cut ribbons to
dedicate fine monuments to their goodness.

I suddenly realized that public acclaim for
generosity is a block to God's blessing.

Charity done in secret opens the floodgates
to God's blessings. (Mal. 3:10).

Art Fettig

Perhaps this secret is but a variation of the Golden Rule, "Do unto others as you might have them do unto you."

Of course the Golden Rule may be found in most books of faith. In the Bible it is found in Matthew 7:12. "Whatsoever you will that men would do to you, do so to them; for this is the law of the Prophets."

Buddhism has it in Udanvarga 5:18, "Hurt not others in ways that you yourself would find harmful."

Hinduism says it this way in Mahabharata 5:1517, "This is the sum of duty; do naught unto others which would cause you pain if done to you."

Islam's Sunan says, "Not one of you is a believer until he desires for his brother that which he desires for himself."

The Book of Mormon states in Alma 42:14, "Therefore, my son, see that you are merciful unto your brethren: deal justly, judge righteously, and do good continually; and if ye do all these things then shall ye receive your reward."

And the Jewish faith finds it in Talmud Shathat 31a, "What is hateful to you, do not to your fellow man. That is the entire Law: all the rest is commentary."

Now if the Golden Rule is so important that it is found in virtually every major religion, then why could not an enhancement of the Golden Rule be even more powerful?

Our modification might read, "Do unto others as you would have them do unto you, even when you know they are unable to return your generosity and, in fact, obtain a promise from them that under no circumstance will they endeavor to repay you in any way."

"And do unto others in secret. Then do it even more generously by swearing yourself and the other party to secrecy of your good deed."

By so doing we have now created something, perhaps, superior to the Golden Rule. Let us call it "The Platinum Rule."

The Golden Rule calls for an equal return, where our Platinum Rule is capable of creating a result that will amaze you.

Like that unskilled stone mason who became a world renowned sculptor; like that disinterested doctor who became one of the world's greatest surgeons; you too might have a breakthrough in your career that will bring you great fame and fortune.

How do I know this? Because, although I have just begun to seriously test this formula myself, the results are already overwhelming.

In some areas my talents have increased tenfold and at the same time my business skills are producing results that I have never experienced before in my lifetime.

The more I learn about the lives of the world's greatest philanthropists, the more convinced I am that they, too, shared the secret of the Platinum Rule.

Most of the world's great foundations were funded by successful people whose wealth increased a hundredfold again and again and again.

If you will study their lives and their giving habits you will find evidence that secret works of charity played an important part in their lives.

Many not only gave of their fortunes, but they gave of their time and their talents as well. And many, as their fortunes grew, contributed more and more and more of their wealth to helping others.

So my friend, I have now shared a great secret with you.

A secret so simple to apply that you will probably say, "It couldn't be much." He might have written it on a small piece of paper with just these few words:

"Find a person in need, exchange a vow of secrecy and understanding that repayment is forbidden, and then fill that need."

I've written these words as I travelled the streets of Madrid and visited the Plazas and the museums. As I sat and studied many of the finest paintings in the world, I wondered about the rare talents that had produced those masterpieces.

As I walked the streets and enjoyed viewing the famous sculptures, I wondered if maybe, many of the greatest talents of all times might have been enhanced by this secret of the Platinum Rule.

The slot machine I played in the Spanish town of Tauvillo at Las Ciguenas was fun, but it was quite tame compared with the daily joy and wonder that comes to those of us who understand and practice the Platinum Rule.

Try it, why don't you, and some day perhaps we will meet. And you will smile, and nod, and wink at me with that look of joy and success glowing on your face as you say, "Ah yes, you too know the secret of the Platinum Rule."

Epilogue

You might wonder if I might be breaking or at least threatening to break my own vow of secrecy in sharing with you the very fact that I am now practicing the Platinum Rule. I think not.

I have revealed none of the details. I write this book for no personal glory. I write this book because I feel obligated to share with all humankind this powerful lesson.

I take no responsibility for the results you might encounter once you decide to use this secret in your own life.

As Lloyd Douglas explained in his own book **Dr. Hudson's Secret Journal,** some readers wrote him that they had tried the formula in their lives and failed. I can only attest to my own discoveries.

Shortly after reading **Magnificent Obsession,** I was presented with a perfect opportunity to practice the formula. I ignored the principles.

I loaned a friend two thousand dollars to meet the down payment on a home he dearly wanted to buy for his family. I failed to give the money freely but instead made it a loan to be repaid without interest at my friend's convenience. I did not exchange a vow of secrecy. Thereafter, every time I saw that friend I thought about my two thousand dollars and the fact that my friend had made no effort at repayment of the loan.

On a number of occasions, I mentioned to other friends that I had made that loan. I know now that I cheated myself and my friend badly. Just think, if I had practiced the Platinum Rule, every time I saw my friend, I would hold our secret in my heart and feel an unbridled joy.

God works in many mysterious ways in our lives but why not give him a little help?

Practicing the Platinum Rule is one way, and believe me, it is the source of untold returns of talent, wealth and personal happiness.

Open up your heart and your life to God's blessings.

About The Author

*A*rt Fettig was born in Detroit, Michigan July 5, 1929. In 1960 he moved with his family to Battle Creek, Michigan, where he now resides. He married Ruthie, his wife of over thirty-eight years and she died of cancer , June 26, 1993. They have four grown children and four grandchildren.

Art Fettig began writing professionally in 1961 and he has thirty-five books published, including *How To Hold An Audience In The Hollow Of Your Hand, The Three Robots* series of children's stories, *The Platinum Rule* and *Love Is The Target.*

He began working in the safety field in early 1948. And spent thirty-five years in the railroad industry, working first as a claim agent investigating thousands of tragic accidents. Then, for ten years, he dedicated his efforts to preventing such accidents. His award winning audio visual programs on safety have been seen by millions of students throughout the United States and Canada.

During the Korean conflict, Fettig served as a combat rifleman in the United States Army. He was wounded in combat and awarded *The Military Order of The Purple Heart..*

He is the founder of Growth Unlimited Inc., a corporation dedicated to bringing positive living concepts to people.

In 1963 he began his career as a professional speaker and has made presentations in all of the fifty states, eight Canadian provinces, and several foreign locations including Malaysia and Hong Kong. He is now a veteran of well over 4,000 professional presentations.

Today, Art Fettig spends a great deal of time writing and speaking in the fields of safety and motivation. He is especially active in the power, petrol, and construction fields. He is often featured as a keynoter at major conventions.

In 1980 he was certified as a "Speaking Professional" (CSP) by the National Speaker's Association. Art continues to write and lecture on personal growth, positive attitude and change. Author of eight children's books, he is a frequent visitor to elementary schools where he speaks for students on "Saying Yes To Positive Living."

Art Fettig is featured in over fifty video programs on safety, sales, motivation, and positive attitudes. He is also featured on several audio cassette programs.

Art has the unique ability to reach people of all backgrounds and of all ages with his spellbinding messages. He's a popular convention keynoter and is in constant demand by major corporations to speak for all of their employees, including blue collar workers and top management groups.

Art Fettig may be contacted at Growth Unlimited Inc., 36 Fairview Ave, Battle Creek, Michigan, 49017. Phone toll-free at 1-800-441-7676 or (616) 965-2229. The Fax number is (616) 965-4522.

Or Email at: artfettig@voyager.net

Go Platinum!

With
"Mr. Platinum"

Art Fettig

Author of
The Platinum Rule

"If You Aren't Giving You Aren't Living."

Go Platinum!
A theme you can build a great meeting or an entire convention around.

Go Platinum With Commitment!

Reach a new level of
commitment to your profession.

Go Platinum With Sales!

Learn some of the secrets of the
Masters In Selling.

Go Platinum with Giving!

If you aren't giving you aren't living.
Learn how to put this powerful message to work
for greater success and happiness.

Go Platinum With Your Whole Life!

Platinum business, personal, spiritual and
financial growth can be yours. Start today.
Learn how to begin this adventurous journey.

Art Fettig is a catalyst for change. He touches people's lives and makes them better. Veteran of over 3,000 professional presentations in all 50 of the United States and 8 Canadian Provinces, his live programs, his 37 books, his hundreds of published articles, his audio-visual products have had a major impact on the lives of thousands.

His client list includes many of the major corporations and associations in the U.S. and Canada, including General Motors, DuPont, the United States Air Force, the United States Navy, Exxon and British Petroleum.

A humorist-motivational speaker, Art Fettig served in the United States Army in the Korean Conflict as a combat rifleman where he was wounded and awarded the *Military Order Of The Purple Heart.*

Hire this powerful speaker for your next important meeting, conference or convention.

Humor!
Motivation!
Inspiration!

Contact Art Fettig at:

Growth Unlimited Inc.
36 Fairview Ave, Battle Creek, MI 49017
(616) 965-2229 (800) 441-7676
Fax: (616) 965-4522
Email: artfettig@voyager.net
Website: www.IMASource.com

Go Platinum

G	Giving - If you aren't giving you aren't living.
O	Ongoing - Learning is a lifetime pursuit.
P	Passion - You must develop a passion for your profession, or professionalism.
L	Love - Love is the target. That is our entire mission and the more you tie that mission in with your profession the more you will soar.
A	An attitude of gratitude - Develop the daily habit of counting our blessings and then watch them grow.
T	Tenacity - You must cultivate the tenacity of a bulldog, one that will enable you to bite a hole in the side of a battleship.
I	Invest - Your time, your money, your talents in personal growth and in sharing that growth with others.
N	Networking - Cultivate the very best professional in each field in your community and develop a system of mutual selling.
U	Unconventional - Become more creative. Find out what everyone else is doing and then do something different.
M	Mentoring - Seek out a mentor who is at the very top of your field. As you develop your success then share it with others along the way. The ultimate in learning comes from the process of teaching others.

Go Platinum!
Seek the next level and then the level after that.
Remember, that success is not a destination,
it is an exciting adventure.

"I have been editing the tapes from the General Sessions, and I have been struck over and over again with how deeply you affected the audience, and how responsive they were to you. You wowed 'em at the Masters."

Mike Pallin, Floyd Wickman's Master Sales Academy.

Art Fettig's Inspirational Products
Books and Tapes That May Touch Your Life

Platinum Rule

The powerful secret to attaining great wealth and happiness. Thousands sold by word of mouth.

Paperback Edition $7.95
Audio Tape $9.95

Mentor: Secret of the Ages

You will be introduced to your own personal "mentor," your "friend in need" in time of crisis. Whenever you want you'll be able to turn to this written masterpiece for guidance and comfort.

Hardcover Autographed Edition $9.95
Paperback Edition $5.95
Audio Tape $9.95

Serenity! Serenity! Living The Serenity Prayer

One man's quest for serenity, acceptance and courage. A must for those in recovery or anyone seeking joy.
Paperback $5.95

Love is the Target
An Answer for Troubled Americans Today

This little book will provide you with the answer you seek to live a happier, healthier, more productive life.
Paperback $5.95

Now Available in Audio and Video Tapes
This funny, fun and inspirational presentation captures all of the joy and high energy of a live performance.

Love is the Target Video $39.95   Audio Tape $9.95
Special-Get All Three: Book, Audio & Video for just $40.00

Attention Professional Speakers and Toastmasters

Three All New Videos Created Especially for Speakers

See Art Fettig, C.S.P. live in the comfort of your own home or listen to him on tape in your car.

In Hawaii Art Fettig made 3 incredible videos just for speakers. Let an expert show you how it is really done on these sensational videos.

Becoming a Professional Speaker Art Fettig speaks for members of the Hawaiian Chapter of the National Speakers Association about turning a part-time writing hobby into a full-time speaking career.

From Toastmasters to Rain Forests on Maui A personal session on speaking with Art Fettig, in the rain forest on Maui. How to build a professional speech 5 to 7 minutes at a time.

Making $2,000 to $20,000 a Day (By Using Your Talents) Another one to one session with Art Fettig on money, commitment and success.

Fantastic Combination Offer

Get all Three Combinations at a Remarkable Savings

Add the Karaoke Video and SAVE EVEN MORE

Yes, we'd like you to benefit from all of our products created for parents and children. You receive all three combinations, *The Three Robots Say Yes Kit* (a $35.20 value), *The Three Robots Success Course* (a $48.05 value), and the *Pos Parenting Package* (a $33.90 value), a total retail value of $120.15, all for just $79.95, plus $5 shipping. (PRC-2) *When you buy the complete package we will include an attractive vinyl 8-pack album for the tapes.* Unfortunately, today, most people learn about success and happiness in some form of a rehabilitation program, that is, if they survive. The question you must ask yourself is this, "Do I want my children to learn that they are special, wonderful, unique individuals now, or do I want them to discover it after they have really made a mess of their lives?" This combination of great, life changing ideas and techniques are yours for the asking at a price anyone can afford.

Buy the Yes Kit, Success Kit, Parenting Kit & Yes Karaokees for $99.95

Add the Karaoke Video (a $29.95 value) for only $20 more when you buy this special combination offer

Call us at 1-800-441-7676 right now and get started immediately on a success program that will not only touch your child's life, but yours as well.

Call us at 800 441-7676 Today!

The
Three Robots

The Three Robots "Just Say Yes" Kit

The Three Robots *"Just Say Yes"* Kit is great for parents to use in the home with their children. It can be used in classrooms too. Thousands of children have already benefited from this powerful program. Don't Delay! *Order Now.*

> The Three Robots-Book and Tape
> The Three Robots Learn About Drugs-Book and Tape
> The New Just Say Yes Activity Book
> The Just Say Yes Rap & Somebody Tape

> A $36.20 Value... Special - Just $29.95
> (CHYK-1)

The Three Robots Success Kit

Why wait until your children grow up and accidentally stumble upon success concepts? Teach them now about success and happiness. As a bonus you will learn these powerful success principles as you share them with your children.

> The Three Robots Find a Grandpa-Book & Tape
> The Three Robots and the Sandstorm-Book & Tape
> The Three Robots Discover Their Pos-Abilities-Book & Tape
> Remembering-Book & Tape
> The Three Robots Activity Book
> 10 Pos Stickers, an Achievement Card & "I'm a Pos" Pin

> Everything Above! A $50.05 Value - Just $39.95
> (CHSK-1)

The Three Robots Books & Tapes Sold Individually

> Books......................$3.95
> Work Books..............$6.95
> Tapes.......................$5.95